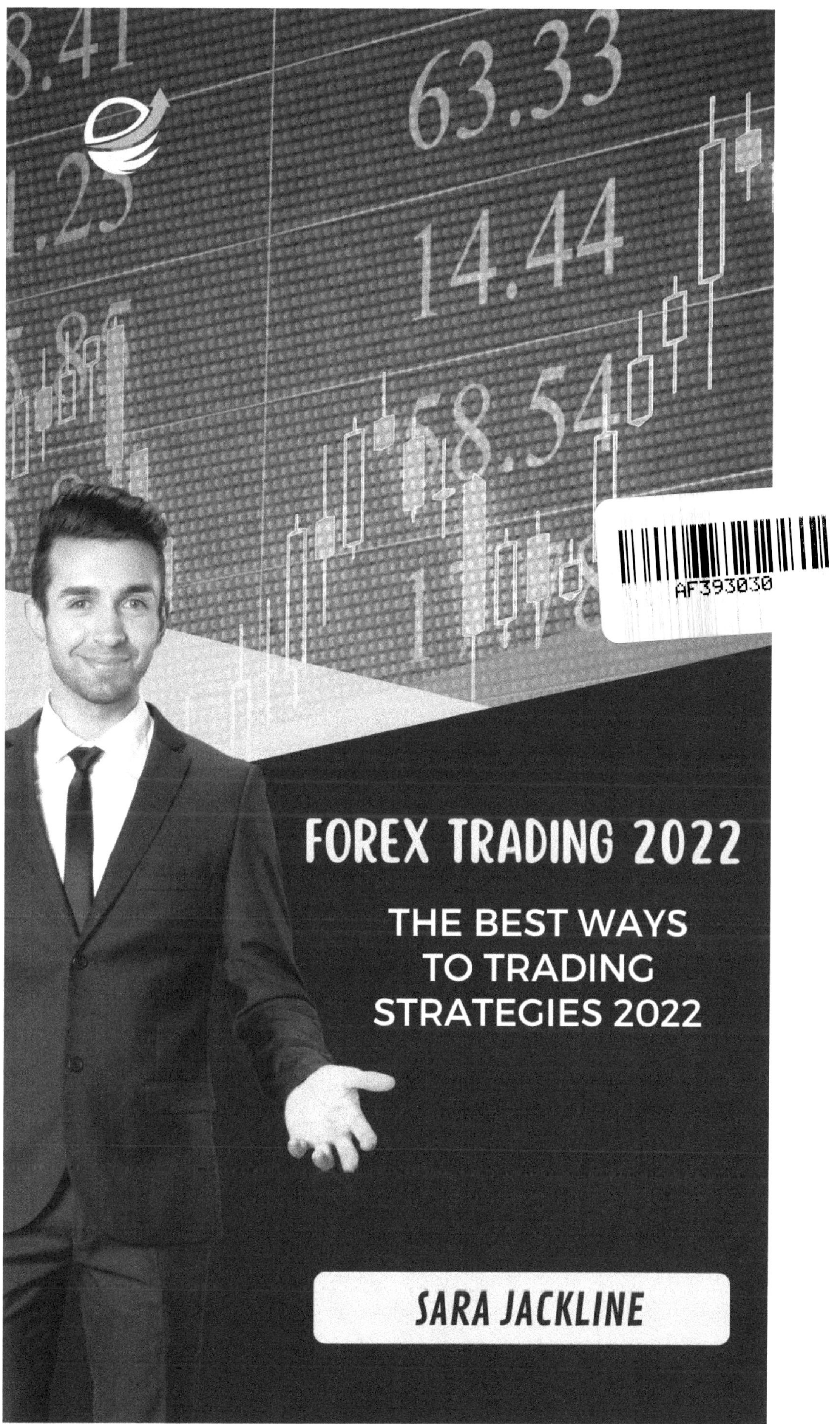
63.33
14.44
8.54
FOREX TRADING 2022
THE BEST WAYS TO TRADING STRATEGIES 2022
SARA JACKLINE

Forex Trading 2022:

The Best Ways To Trading Strategies 2022

* The Forex market Trading 2022

It is everyone's dream to make pay simply through sitting at a PC of their domestic and spending insignificant undertakings. Trading shares from your house is an interesting different alternative that allows you to have your privately settled enterprise and stay this dream. You get greater open doorways whilst operating from domestic, do not want to answer to a prevalent, have greater time with own circle of relatives, and bring an installment through basically putting in or 3 hours in the back of a PC. Your hours are flexible relying upon the kind of trades you're awaiting to carry out and furthermore the protections exchange hours.

You can pass as much less as an hour each day to so long as the entire day gambling out the sum of your exam and placing trades.

With the advances in improvement and web, buying and selling as a enterprise has gotten extensively simpler and with some snaps in your PC you'll land up being a inventory cash associated professional. You can in like way display symptoms and symptoms of development yield in your speculation due to the parcel greater low priced charges for agents. The pastime of stockbrokers and institutions as pass-betweens is faded impressively.

There are diverse picks available for on line center humans with exclusive businesses and charges.

Considering your enterprise frameworks and spending, you may select out from a aggregate of on line government open. With digital buying and selling, you moreover discard all of the paintings vicinity paintings associated with the inventory buying and selling. You can get in your report securely thru the Internet together along with your non-public thriller country and buying and selling is simply numerous snaps away.

One little bit of leeway of buying and selling as a enterprise is that now no longer ordinary for diverse institutions you do not want to location significant proportions of cash in it to start. Such a enterprise would not require a modern sport plan, area rental, laborers, and a significant shop to preserve up the enterprise. You have to genuinely have a PC with an Internet affiliation, a report, and primary records at the budgetary exchange and coins.

The attainable pay in buying and selling a enterprise may be as excessive as 100K every year and altogether greater for professionals and pros. You can in like way produce vital repayment through extending your portfolio and organizing productively. Essentially make multiple frameworks and keep on with them.

Do some thing it takes now no longer to permit feelings keep you up of purchasing or promoting shares. This is the maximum big aspect in getting possible on this enterprise and having the opportunity to manipulate your peril and return.

Like beginning a few exclusive enterprise, you have to be tranquil and extraordinarily efficient whilst buying and selling shares as a enterprise. There are many getting prepared projects, on line guides, and automatic books that will let you with remodeling right into a efficient inventory dealer and professional capacities predicted to make your enterprise a beneficial one.

In like way, there are numerous digital making plans applications which could make the direction closer to buying and selling much less complicated through giving precise exam and blueprints to shop time for your enterprise and to make buying and selling understood.

* the Forex market Trading

A enterprise may be basically characterised as a motion this is finished for gain. The precept assessment among sporting on a enterprise and a aspect hobby is that a enterprise has a preference for the gain, is administered in a precise, chronic and standard manner, consists of the computation of costs and risks covered, and consists of making projections of earning and profit. Thus, the Forex market replacing is enterprise because the number one goal of maximum agents is to create enjoy the marketplace. Truth be told, the Forex market replacing may be considered as the appropriate enterprise for any person who isn't kidding approximately it. Here are ten motives why.

1. THE ABILITY TO START SMALL

You do not need to have a notable deal of coins to get this enterprise in progress. A smaller than predicted replacing report can essentially be opened for as meager as $250! For a trendy report, as a minimum approximately $2,500 is all this is required. Simply assessment this and the big variety of bucks predicted to start a enterprise.

2. Brief duration COMMITMENT

Any standard enterprise might also additionally count on eight to twelve hours of hard paintings each day. In the Forex market replacing, contingent upon the replacing structures being applied, the time obligation is considerably much less. Best the Forex market sellers spend near 2 to a few hours out of every day replacing the marketplace. In spite of the truth that the the Forex market exhibit is a 24-hour advertisement, there are bunches of strategies with which notable replacing openings may be outstanding with out making an investment broadened instances of strength earlier than the PC. Truth be told, severa powerful traders started replacing whilst on the equal time retaining their day employments but as but making thousands of blessings from the the Forex market put it on the market.

three. Quick RESULTS

A traditional enterprise might also additionally normally take months or maybe a totally long term to start yielding outcomes. In the problem of the Forex market replacing, blessings may be visible in most effective a short time-frame. When proven and a success replacing strategies are through and huge reliably implemented and with valid coins the executive's requirements, replacing blessings could be produced whilst the capabilities to gain from this marketplace could likewise increment.

4. NO OVERHEADS AND STUFF

There may be no trouble of coping with team of workers turnover, place of job troubles, workplace rental, inventory, and big quantities of various overheads in a monotonous enterprise. the Forex market replacing simply calls for a PC with a mean Internet affiliation.

Exchanging have to also be feasible on a mobileular telecellsmartphone making it particularly high-quality and convenient.

five. LIQUIDITY

The the Forex market exhibit is the largest economic marketplace at the planet, with what will be in comparison to greater than $three trillion being exchanged each day, whilst the extent of the monetary exchanges is simply around $500 billion. Truth be told, the the Forex market exhibit is greater than the shares, securities, and fates markets joined!

A profoundly fluid marketplace like this allows traders to go into and go away the marketplace effectively, with the marketplace now no longer having the choice to be managed through any person. This implies a degree gambling subject is made for retail traders to gain from.

6. Unpredictability

Because of its out and out liquidity, the the Forex market exhibit is particularly unpredictable, introducing diverse replacing probabilities to put it on the market members. High instability could result in ordinary wonderful styles that may be stuck with the perfect methodologies. The cxccssive instability withinside the the Forex market exhibit allows the maximum blessings to be produced the use of wonderful styles contrasted with replacing shares, alternatives, and fates.

7. Influence

On account of the depth of affect, the earnings produced from replacing the the Forex market put it on the market some distance outperform the ones in standard ventures. In spite of the truth that affect moreover makes severa undeveloped sellers lose coins rapidly, so long as green danger manage methodologies are visible with discipline, affect can paintings for, instead of in opposition to you.

eight. Absence OF PHYSICAL EXCHANGE

The absence of a bodily exchange withinside the the Forex market put it on the market empowers it to paintings on a 24-hour premise, crossing beginning with one-time place then onto the following over the predominant cash associated focuses, for example, Sydney, Hong Kong, Tokyo, Frankfurt, London, New York, and so forth. As it's far a 24-hour exhibit, daily replacing schedules may be organized to such an volume that they do not meddle with different normal exercises, specifically an all-day paintings and different own circle of relatives unit responsibilities.

9. LOW TRANSACTION COSTS

Most the Forex market intermediaries do not rate a fee for exchanges entered thru their foundation. The rate of replacing hence originates from the unfold among the provide and ask charges. Exchanging costs may be saved low through essentially targeting replacing cash units wherein the unfold is as skinny as will be predicted below the circumstances. In any case, this is based upon the strategies being applied too. A few strategies are greater a success whilst applied on crosses that have a greater big unfold.

10. Value STABILITY

To wrap matters up, due to the excessive liquidity of the the Forex market exhibit, charges are continually steady. This implies big positions may be achieved at an inexpensive value.

So as to be extraordinarily powerful in the Forex market replacing, it ought to be taken a gander at as a enterprise (which it's far, at any rate) in preference to a diversion.

This implies there ought to be good enough hypothesis of time and coins to have the choice to ace the capabilities to change, whilst concurrently exercise notable coins the board requirements and directing possible cash-saving gain exam, plenty similar to retaining a standard enterprise.

* Treat Your the Forex market Trading Like A Business

This file will deal with a notable deal of the giant factors that the Forex market traders absolutely must consciousness on. Significant additives primarily based totally across the vital factors are given so that you could have the choice to middle to enhance your replacing mind science.

Focus at the noteworthy zones.

the Forex market replacing is tied in with bringing in coins. It is secure to mention which you are pulling coins from the enterprise sectors or could you are saying you're giving your property to the geniuses? Ideally, it's far the excellent alternative. It is essential that your giant time is spent operating at stable structures you'll have the choice to complete on with little postponement to channel your the Forex market coping with to a greater efficient and low-priced degree. In this regard there are numerous agents on this tough spot, questioning that its tough to benefit a sort of enjoy the enterprise sectors and trying to find hearty strategies to offer their development at the song toward dependable gainfulness. One of the primary troubles you have to consciousness on is managing your replacing as a enterprise - now no longer an hobby. In the occasion that your replacing is being taken into consideration as a pastime, at that factor you'll maximum probable lose your property.

Everything begins offevolved with the the Forex market replacing plan.

To begin any enterprise you need to have a strategy. Conveying a pre-characterised the Forex market replacing application is an immensely giant factor toward making improvements to your replacing. Productive enterprise endeavors aren't, extensively, labored with out a stable association, and replacing could be cautioned to be tended to love a enterprise. It is pivotal that you'll have the choice to reply to each unmarried conceivable scenario that floor whilst replacing request to acquire a high-quality conclusive final results and toughen your replacing. A enterprise subject has set responsibilities that allows you to deal with all opportunities as this diminishes suspecting time whilst an event happens and prevents any vagueness.

A the Forex market replacing enterprise requests the supplier has a sturdy association permitting each unmarried indistinct selection to be expelled at the off threat that it's far to make a predictable gain. It is possibly appreciably greater giant withinside the the Forex market exhibit than a few different exclusive enterprise, to suggest all additives of your focal predominant affiliation with the the Forex market put it on the market - since right here untruths the rudimentary strategies for seeing you do not clasp below tension. Do you change the EURUSD news? It is secure to mention which you are a swing broker? Be express approximately your association.

These are multiple the errors fledgling traders are slanted to make:

- Contributing greater property to dropping positions.

- Embarking on below trendy exchanges with least or 0 association.

- No focus of event danger.

- Hurrying into positions after a time-frame outdoor the enterprise sectors.

- Engaging with the marketplace with little relaxation or below pressure.

- Bad or non-existent coins the executive's strategies.

- Skipping from one replacing association of regulations to an exchange one.

How do professional agents deal with similar situations of troubles?

- Scaling into exchanges with becoming coins the board

- Having exclusive the Forex market traders on hand at the off threat that one is unavailable

- All of the timekeeping down for the precise framework change ideas the front of coming into a position.

- Following the enterprise region perception and focus of event threat presentation.

- Having downtime whilst debilitated or now no longer at their excellent.

* Commodity Trading for Beginners

Generally, constructing a hypothesis portfolio has covered retaining aid classes: shares and bonds but in recent times greater monetary professionals are seeking to gadgets to make bigger their portfolio and provide turbo-charged improvement.

In the prevailing article, we see what is largely gadgets 101. We will cowl a few essential phrases which might be applied withinside the realm of product replacing in order that withinside the following article we can "hit the floor running" and start to discover approximately structures for replacing gadgets.

The first and maximum clean inquiry to reply is what are wares? also, the right reaction is extraordinarily primary - A product is any bodily substance exchanged at the potentialities exchange. Some diverse styles of wares include Orange Juice, Oil, Gold, and Unleaded Gasoline.

A greater mind-boggling query to reply is the way to change merchandise?

Throughout the subsequent three articles, I will inform you the excellent manner to element a few essential object replacing strategies.

Before making your preliminary rarely any merchandise exchanges it's far primary to look a few vital phraseology grow to be familiar with numerous essential requirements:

Set up and realise your danger profile.

Be organized to withdraw feeling out of your replacing picks.

I do not get my that means through constructing up and know-how your danger profile? Basically, you must pick out what number of dangers you're glad to take and absolutely realise the risks related to the diverse styles of product replacing strategies open to the retail speculator. Ware replacing makes use of to apply and may be unstable. You have to simply make a contribution danger capital and must be installation to lose what you make a contribution if the change would not workout the way in that you expected that it have to. On the off threat that this sounds excessively risky for you, at that factor possibly ware replacing isn't always for you.

In the occasion which you are as but perusing and aren't reeling on the possibility of dropping coins at that factor, it is a really perfect possibility to speak about the second one giant trendy. The feeling has no spot in any object replacing procedure. An powerful ware supplier can isolate themselves completely from their feelings and make valid, knowledgeable picks approximately whilst to buy an object and all of the greater giant whilst to promote.

Since you've got got made it beyond the preliminary scarcely any passages are as but eager on replacing merchandise we are able to start to take a gander at a few vital phrases which you have to recognise earlier than you may make your first ware exchanges; name picks and placed alternatives.

Call Options

A name opportunity is a preference that offers the holder the privilege but now no longer the dedication to buy the primary ware at a foreordained value on the very contemporary a fixcd cxpiry date.

To realise what this means in greater vital phrases how approximately we use Pizza Hut as our model. Envision that a pepperoni pizza is ordinarily $10 but there may be an fantastic coupon that allows the holder to pay simply $eight for the same pizza. In our similarity, the coupon is a name preference and the Pizza is the ware. The coupon has an estimation of $2 in mild of the truth that it allows the holder to buy a $10 pizza for simply $eight. Presently how approximately we envision that there may be an expiry date on our coupon and at the off threat that we've got now no longer applied it through that date, at that factor it not has any worth.

Put Options

A placed preference is a preference that offers the client the privilege but now no longer the dedication to promote the hidden ware at a foreordained value previous to a fixed expiry date.

In reality, we have to envision a telecellsmartphone keep is doing a repurchase application for Samsung Galaxy phones at $220 but to make use of the development you want to expose the voucher earlier than a particular date. Utilizing this similarity the Galaxy telecellsmartphone is the object and the voucher is the placed opportunity. Presently how approximately we envision that some other keep is promoting a recycled Galaxy telecellsmartphone at $one hundred seventy. You can promote the telecellsmartphone which you simply bought for $one hundred seventy at $220, a gain of $50. This is the estimation of the voucher.

In the subsequent article, we are able to check out a few essential product methodologies. Up to that factor, it is a really perfect possibility to make certain you understand approximately the rudiments we've got shrouded in this text and put together to make some blessings withinside the energizing universe of product change.

* What Is Commodity Trading?

Product replacing is a contributing approach that consists of shopping and promoting of wares. Products are characterised as some thing this is considered as worth, has a best this is normalized, and is introduced in big sums.

At the factor whilst people placed assets into gadgets, they for the maximum component suppose as some distance as 'merchandise' which might be property that is probably sold for a huge scope of employment. For instance, metals whether or not treasured or non-treasured, are considered as conscious and exchanged primarily based totally at the huge scope of products that may be created making use of them as a key fixing.

Who places assets into Commodity Trading?

Ads: Entities engaged with the creation, handling, or advertising of focus. In product replacing, each the rancher and the enterprise as an instance ITC (the principle FMCG firm), which obtains wheat from the ranchers, will be named as substances.

Speculators: A collecting of monetary professionals that pool their coins collectively to decrease danger and increment again.

Retail Investors: Individual object sellers who change on their very own facts or thru a product service provider to make the most the fee changes.

Why Commodities Trading?

Items are the principle aid magnificence this is adversely related to bonds, making them a essential tool for broadening. As a rule, bonds are simply negligibly related with shares, but merchandise have absolutely been adversely associated with the 2 shares and bonds generally. As such, whilst shares and bonds increment, wares will in wellknown lessening.

How Commodities Trading functions?

State, at the off threat which you want to make the most growing gold charges, and glaringly higher route is to place assets into gold by using gold potentialities from the goods exchange in preference to absolutely placing off to the marketplace and getting it.

Most definitely, you try 3 matters.

1. Purchase the degree of gold decided withinside the settlement.

2. Get it on the value decided withinside the settlement.

three. Get it at the expiry of the settlement. This will be the subsequent one month or greater.

Pre-necessities of Commodity Trading

So as to change merchandise, you have to to start with discover approximately settlement determinations of each unmarried ware as ordered through the exchange, and glaringly discover approximately replacing structures. Nuts and bolts preserve as earlier than as a few different challenge - buy low and promote excessive.

Much similar to fee replacing, Investors are required to open an replacing account with a consultant or sub-service provider; facts putting in deal with and individual affirmation are required. While professionals shift at the reviews required for verification, maximum call for a PAN card as affirmation of photo personality. Ledger subtleties are moreover asked empowering agreement and installment.

* Commodity Trading Strategies

Items are products this is in huge hobby and are absolutely constant and do not assessment plenty concerning best. For instance, gold may be gold whether or not it is mined in Africa or Australia.

In mild of this norm in best, this products turns into treasured contraptions for hypothesis and replacing. At the factor while you buy a barrel of unrefined petroleum, as an instance, you recognise what you are getting and also you may not get scammed or cheated.

Instances of products and gadgets that may be exchanged as merchandise consist of:

* Precious metals, for example, gold, silver, and copper.

* Agricultural gadgets, for example, elastic, corn, rice, and sugar.

* Energy and cutting-edge property, for example, uncooked petroleum, coal, and aluminum.

* Non-standard "property". Innovative people have began discussing "regular

capital" and replacing carbon outflows
and climate.

Exchanging Commodities

At the factor whilst people speak approximately replacing merchandise, maximum of them aren't absolutely getting one ton of sugar and in a while promoting it seven days after the truth.

Products are frequently exchanged making use of subsidiary devices, for example, potentialities. Purchasing a fates settlement of a hidden ware implies you're shopping the choice to buy the product at a particular value at a particular destiny date. Meanwhile, the actual value of the object is going throughout each day. This vacillation makes the potentialities agreement both pass up or down in value contingent upon which bearing the essential object's value is going.

The Commodity Market

Items are exchanged universally and are exchanged on exclusive trades the arena over. Instances of those include the Chicago Mercantile Exchange, Australian Securities Exchange, and the Tokyo Commodity Exchange. These trades pass approximately as industrial facilities wherein object potentialities agreements may be exchanged and labored out.

The charges of gadgets upward thrust and fall. Some are recurrent, whilst others depend on the cutting-edge economic viewpoint and political situations. For instance, the value of horticultural gadgets like corn and rice varies depending upon the season, and moreover at the year's collection.

Then again, gadgets, for example, unrefined petroleum are reliant on monetary and political circumstances. For instance, if there may be political shakiness, for example, battle or authorities troubles withinside the

Middle East (wherein a huge part of the oil makers are), the value of uncooked petroleum could upward thrust. Furthermore, the value could upward thrust if the economic system and enterprise are stable, and energy usage is excessive; and the alternative manner around.

Why change Commodities?

The repeating and drifting natures of gadgets provide monetary professionals the threat to change ware fates.

Speculators can procure from replacing product fates through having the choice to foresee the cycles and benefitting throughout monetary and political changes.

Ware potentialities can likewise be exchanged to fence in opposition to the possibility that the primary object would not create an expected yield withinside the cutting-edge cycle. Organizations whose enterprise consists of the ones wares could then fence in opposition to that and acquire a few coins from object fates notwithstanding the truth that their gadgets do not promote well.

For monetary professionals and easygoing agents, product replacing speaks to some other approach for replacing apart from gives or cash.

The risks and prizes are comparative, separated through the essential gadgets being exchanged.

On the off threat which you are eager on product change, you have to perform a little exam at the object you want to pay attention on, and smash down how its value shifts depending upon every year cycles too and political and monetary changes.

* Online Commodity Trading Courses

The universe of ware replacing is inconceivably exclusive and gives severa new and energizing open doorways for replacing. Exchanging wares empower people to partake in expansive marketplace movements or internal express areas. Countless people are eager at the frequently growing ware to put it on the market and henceforth there are faculties that provide exclusive guides in on line ware replacing. These faculties provide full-time guides in object replacing and there are some faculties that appreciably provide guides that preserve going for multiple days.

Online object replacing guides teach people in all elements of the product replacing subject, with the help of maximum latest contraptions and programming. Individuals can determine out the way to installed and manage their very own requests withinside the product exhibit with the help of statistics picked up from those guides. Ware replacing practise carries identifying how the professionals on this subject have coins and the impact among the diverse agreements and divisions replacing. These guides make people prepared for concluding that is a gainful challenge for them and which speculations are higher stayed farfar from through giving them which exchanges consist of an outstanding degree of danger. Various forms of agreements withinside the product marketplace may be applied as one, as those agreements provide substantial affect contingent upon the object being exchanged. These guides likewise provide steerage on which wares are exchanged 24/five and that have constrained timespan. In primary phrases, on line product replacing guides teach people to change with discipline, a useful association, and specialised devices. They consciousness on primary and specialised traits of object replacing.

These guides provide thorough and professional practise this is affordable for newbies and propelled traders.

These guides provide improved simply as intending with education applications and regularly keep in mind communique with absolutely the excellent sellers for the nation.

These sellers assist with studying all of the confusion related to the object marketplace and help college students with constructing up the capability of danger the board thru the order and capital safeguarding.

Coaches are on hand to manipulate in all elements of product practise.

SARA

JACKLINE